RAND

Long-Term Economic and Military Trends 1994–2015

The United States and Asia

Charles Wolf, Jr., K. C. Yeh,
Anil Bamezai, Donald P. Henry,
Michael Kennedy

*Prepared for the
Office of the Secretary of Defense*

**National Defense
Research Institute**

PREFACE

This report presents estimates, for the period from 1994 through 2015, of certain key economic and military trends in Asia that will affect the region's future security environment. Employing a common methodology, separate estimates were made for China and Taiwan by K. C. Yeh; the United States by Michael Kennedy; Japan by Charles Wolf, Jr.; Korea by Donald P. Henry; and India by Anil Bamezai. The methodology and structure of the report follows closely on those reported in earlier RAND work (Charles Wolf, Jr., Gregory Hildebrandt, Michael Kennedy, Donald P. Henry, Katsuaki Terasawa, K. C. Yeh, Benjamin Zycher, Anil Bamezai, and Toshiya Hayashi, *Long-Term Economic and Military Trends, 1950–2010*, Santa Monica, Calif.: RAND, N-2757-USDP, 1989).

The research reported here is part of RAND's project on *Long-Term Trends and the Future Security Environment* for the Director of Net Assessment in the Office of the Secretary of Defense and should be of interest to those concerned with defense and foreign policy, as well as international economic policy. This research was performed in the International Security and Defense Policy Center within RAND's National Defense Research Institute, a federally funded research and development center sponsored by the Office of the Secretary of Defense, the Joint Staff, and the defense agencies.

CONTENTS

Preface   iii

Figures   vii

Tables   ix

Summary   xi

Chapter One
LONG-TERM TRENDS AND THE FUTURE SECURITY
    ENVIRONMENT IN ASIA   1

Chapter Two
PRINCIPAL RESULTS   5
Gross Domestic Product   6
Per-Capita GDP   10
Military Spending   11
Military Capital Stocks   14

Chapter Three
CONCLUDING OBSERVATIONS   19

Appendix: METHODS AND DATA SOURCES   23

Bibliography   53

FIGURES

1. Gross Domestic (National) Products of Selected
   Countries, 1994–2015 9
2. Per-Capita GDPs of the United States and Selected
   Countries 12
3. Military Spending Estimates 15
4. Military Capital Stocks of the United States and
   Selected Countries 18

TABLES

1. Gross Domestic (National) Products of Selected
   Countries 1994–2015   8
2. 1994 Populations and 1994–2015 Population Growth
   Rates of Selected Countries   10
3. Per-Capita GDPs of the United States and Selected
   Countries   11
4. Military Spending Estimates   14
5. Military Capital Stocks of the United States and
   Selected Countries   17
A.1. United States: Trend Estimates   31
A.2. Japan: Trend Estimates   34
A.3. Recent Revisions in Services and GDP   36
A.4. Sources of GDP Growth in China, 1985–1990 and
     1994–2015   39
A.5. China: Trend Results (Stable-Growth Scenario)   41
A.6. China: Trend Results (Disrupted-Growth Scenario) . .   41
A.7. Taiwan: Trend Results   44
A.8. Korea: Trend Results (Soft-Landing Scenario)   48
A.9. India: Trend Results   52

The analysis presented in this report estimates trends from 1994 through 2015 using four salient economic and military indicators for five Asian countries (China, Japan, Korea, Taiwan, and India), as well as the United States. The four indicators are gross domestic product (GDP), per-capita GDP, military spending, and military capital stocks. Trends in these indicators, among many others, may reflect significant changes in the security environment in Asia. All of the estimates should be treated with caution because of the many uncertainties, as well as the often arguable assumptions, that underlie the results.

The forecasts of economic and military trends are based on a hierarchically linked model in which GDP is derived from an aggregate national production function for each country; per-capita GDP is calculated by combining the GDP estimates with demographic data for each country; military spending is estimated as a specified (sometimes varying) proportion of GDP; and each country's military capital is estimated as a specified (sometimes varying) proportion of military spending less depreciation of the previously accumulated military capital stock.

All of our estimates are made in purchasing-power-parity (ppp) 1994 dollars. The appendix includes a discussion of the advantages and disadvantages of ppp exchange rates and the reasons for our use of this conversion procedure.

TRENDS IN GDP

Based on calculations and judgments about future inputs of capital and labor, and changes in factor productivity, we estimate that the annual rate of growth in GDP in the United States will average 2.2 percent over the 1994–2015 period. In 1994 dollars, U.S. GDP is 6.7 trillion in 1994 and will reach an estimated level of 10.7 trillion in 2015.

Japan's rate of growth is estimated at 2.6 percent annually over this period. The ratio between the Japanese and U.S. GDPs changes slightly, with Japan's GDP rising during this period from 39 to 42 percent of that of the United States.

In calculating China's GDP, two alternative scenarios were used: (1) a "disrupted-growth" scenario, resulting in an average annual growth of 3 percent in China's GDP over the period, and (2) a "stable-growth" scenario, resulting in an average annual GDP growth of 4.9 percent over the 1994–2015 period. In the disrupted-growth scenario, China's GDP rises from a 1994 level of $4.9 trillion in purchasing power parity (ppp) dollar equivalents, to a level of $9 trillion in 2015. In the stable-growth scenario, China's GDP rises from nearly $5 trillion in 1994 to $13.6 trillion in 2015; the latter figure would be approximately 27 percent above that of the United States in that year.

In both China scenarios, the ppp exchange rates that we use are at the high end of rates used by others—for example, the ppp rates used in some World Bank calculations are about half the rates we use. While we recognize the imprecision of all these rates, the reasons that seem to us to justify the ones used in this study are explained in some detail in the appendix.

In estimating GDP for Korea, growth simulations have been based on three scenarios, each involving the arbitrary (and admittedly unrealistic) assumption that reunification occurs in 1995: (1) a "soft-landing" scenario, in which reunification occurs through a peaceful, stable, and mutually accommodating process, resulting in a sustained and high growth rate of 7.9 percent annually; (2) reunification accomplished along lines of the German experience in 1990, in which GDP growth rates are somewhat lower in the initial years but rise thereafter; (3) reunification by war, in which initial growth is negative but rapidly rises in the ensuing years, so that by the second decade of the 21st century, the GDP is approximately the same as that reached in the two preceding scenarios ($2.0 trillion in 1994 ppp dollars). If reunification occurs at a later date—a more realistic premise—we expect that the growth trajectories associated with the three scenarios would still ensue, although their starting point would differ from that posited in our calculations.

Taiwan's GDP, starting at a level of $285 billion in 1994, is estimated to rise by 2015 to $860 billion, at which time its GDP is nearly 10 percent of China's disrupted-growth GDP, but only 6 percent of China's stable-growth GDP. During this period, Taiwan's average annual rate of growth is estimated at 5.4 percent.

India's economy is estimated to maintain a steady and high annual growth rate averaging 5.5 percent over the two decades, assuming that economic liberalization continues. Its GDP is estimated to rise from a level of $1.2 trillion in 1994 to $3.7 trillion in 2015, representing an increase in its GDP from about 46 percent of that of Japan in 1994 to approximately 82 percent by 2015, and from 24 percent of China's GDP in 1994 to 27 percent in 2015.

GDP PER CAPITA

Combining our GDP trend estimates with demographic figures for each country yields several interesting results. The per-capita GDPs of Japan and Taiwan are approximately equal to that of the United States by 2015, ($34 thousand), while Korea's per-capita GDP reaches two-thirds of this level. The per-capita GDP of China rises from 20 percent of that of Japan in 1994 to 30 percent in 2015 under the stable-growth scenario, while remaining at 20 percent of that of Japan in the disrupted-growth scenario. India's per-capita GDP in 2015 reaches only about 70 percent of that of China's per-capita GDP in 1994.

MILITARY SPENDING

In estimating military spending for the United States, we assume that the share of military spending of GDP declines from 4 percent to 3 percent by 1998, in accord with the military spending shares estimated in the *Economic Report of the President, 1994.* Thereafter, we assume the 3 percent share is maintained through 2015. Under these assumptions, military spending in the United States declines from 1994 until 2000 and slowly rises thereafter. As the U.S. GDP grows, military spending falls from its present level of $290 billion to $235 billion in 2000, rising thereafter to $322 billion in 2015.

Two alternative military spending estimates are made for Japan: one in which the military spending share of GDP remains at 1 percent and the second in which that share rises to 3 percent. Accordingly, Japan's military spending rises from its present level to about $45 billion in 2015, and $135 billion in 2015, respectively for the two scenarios. Japan's military spending remains substantially below that of the United States in both the 3 percent and 1 percent scenarios.

China's military spending remains below that of the United States through 2015 in the disrupted-growth scenario, but rises above U.S. military spending by 2006 and thereafter, in the stable-growth scenario.

Taiwan's military spending, currently 9 percent of China's, remains at that proportion if China experiences stable growth; if China's growth is disrupted, Taiwan's military spending rises to twice that proportion.

Korea's military spending, currently somewhat below that of Japan ($20 billion versus $26 billion for Japan in 1994 ppp dollars), approximates that of Japan by the year 2000 and exceeds that of Japan thereafter if Japan's military spending share remains at 1 percent of its GDP. If Japan's military spending increases to 3 percent of its GDP, the resulting military spending appreciably exceeds that of Korea throughout the 1994–2015 period.

India's military spending, currently about $42 billion, reaches a regionally significant scale of $148 billion by 2015, representing over 40 percent of China's military spending in its disrupted-growth scenario, and about 23 percent of China's higher military spending in the stable-growth scenario.

MILITARY CAPITAL STOCKS

For the United States, the value of military capital falls over the 1994–2015 period, because additions to U.S. military capital stocks through procurement and construction are less than the depreciation of previously accumulated stocks. Consequently, the present U.S. military capital stock of $1.1 trillion in 1994 is estimated to fall to about $840 billion by 2015.

Japan's military capital stock increases from 9 percent of that of the United States in 1994 to nearly 20 percent in 2015 if Japan's military spending share remains at 1 percent, and to over half that of the United States by 2015 if Japan's annual military spending share of GDP rises to 3 percent.

Korea's military capital in 2015 remains about 80 percent of Japan's in the latter's 1 percent military spending scenario, falling well below that of Japan in relative terms if Japan increases its military spending to 3 percent of its GDP.

China's military capital becomes dominant in the region and reaches a level at about 55 percent of the U.S. level in 2015 in China's stable-growth scenario, and 37 percent of that of the United States in the disrupted-growth scenario. However, within the Asian region, India may exercise a counterweight to China's apparent dominance. India's military capital rises substantially relative to that of China, reaching by 2015 about 77 percent of China's military capital in the stable-growth scenario, and slightly exceeding that of China in the latter's disrupted-growth scenario.

According to our estimates, Taiwan's military capital increases modestly relative to that of China.

CONCLUDING OBSERVATIONS

Many uncertainties surround our forecasts: uncertainties related to the models we have used, the individual country data and their comparability across countries, and neglect of the possible changes that might ensue in the behavior of countries and their decisionmakers if some of the forecasted trends actually unfold. Paradoxically, some of the forecasts—especially for the later years—might turn out to be wrong because other forecasts—especially for the earlier years—were accurate. For example, if China's military spending and military capital were to move toward the large and perhaps alarming scale of our estimates, the military spending and procurement decisions by other countries, including the United States, might change substantially. In turn, China's anticipation of such a response might exercise downward pressure on its own military allocations. In this sense, our forecasts might turn out to be "self-preventing," rather than "self-fulfilling."

Still other uncertainties are associated with the possible occurrence of major exogenous events—for example, military conflicts or the forging or fracturing of alliances—that might alter the behavior of decisionmakers and the performance of economies.

Another important uncertainty arises from the extent to which the countries for which we have made forecasts might use the noncapital shares (70–75 percent) of their military spending to enhance military effectiveness by innovative changes in military technology, organization, and operations. These issues, which pertain to a revolution in military affairs, are not addressed in this study.

While we acknowledge the numerous uncertainties that apply to our estimates, several inferences can be drawn from them that are relevant to the future security environment in Asia.

1. The long-term trends projected here probably foreshadow over the next two decades a tremendous growth of both economic and military power in the Asian region relative to that in the rest of the world.

2. Within the Asian region, the parities among the Asian countries will change significantly, and the disparities among them will grow, both in economic and military terms. China's aggregate economic as well as military capabilities will grow significantly relative to most of the other countries in the region, except India. Yet, the economic well-being of China's populace (as crudely measured by per-capita GDP) will remain substantially below that of most other countries in the region, again with the exception of India.

3. Korea's economic capabilities are likely to grow relative to those of Japan, as will its relative military strength unless Japan increases its military efforts.

4. India is likely to become a more significant actor in the region, in both economic and military terms, and will probably increase in both dimensions relative to China.

5. The economic and military prominence of the United States will remain throughout the region, although its relative scale and scope will diminish.

6. Finally, it remains to be seen whether and how these changes in the relative scale and influence of the *national* actors in the region will be modified or channeled by contemporaneous *transnational* trends—for example, trends in international security alliances, in international business alliances, and in transnational informational and occupational communication and transactions. Such transnational trends have not been considered in the work described here.

Chapter One

LONG-TERM TRENDS AND THE FUTURE SECURITY ENVIRONMENT IN ASIA

The influences that affect the future security environment in Asia, as elsewhere, are numerous and, at least at a broad and general level, familiar. These influences include political, social, technological, historical, and ethnic elements, as well as economic and military ones. What are not well-known, and indeed may be unfathomable, are the relative weight that should be applied to each of these myriad influences and the strength of the interactions among them. Even in retrospect, it is often exceedingly difficult to be precise about the relative weights or the interactions among the forces that were involved in shaping the security environment. For example, it is incontestable that the dissolution of the Soviet Union has had a profound influence on the current, as well as the future, global security environment. Yet, four years after the fact, it remains quite unclear how much of the explanation for this defining event should be attributed to economic or to military or to political influences, to internal or external ones, and to interactions among all of these.

The work summarized in this report focuses on several narrower questions that relate to, but do not directly address, these broader issues. In this work, we assume that the relative economic and military levels of the principal national economies and national military establishments are among the influences that will significantly affect the future security environment in Asia. Proceeding from this assumption, we focus on four salient, highly aggregate indicators—*gross domestic product (GDP), per-capita GDP, military spending,* and *military capital stocks*—and track their trends from 1994 through 2015. While these are not the only factors affecting the future Asian security environment, they are among the important ones. GDP and its growth are admittedly gross, but plausible, indicators of the relative size of the national economies and of changes therein. Per-capita GDP is suggestive of prevailing living standards in the region, and of disparities among the regions. Military spending and military capital are relevant, if only partial, indicators of military capabilities and (perhaps) intentions. For example, the recent Department of Defense assessment of U.S. security strategy in the Asia-Pacific region observes:

> China's published defense budget figure has doubled in the past five years, with real growth—adjusted for inflation—estimated at about 40 percent. This figure probably does not encompass all of China's defense expenditures . . . . Absent a better understanding of China's plans, capabilities and intentions, other Asian nations may feel a need to respond to China's growing military power. (Department of Defense, 1995).

This assessment is also noteworthy because it highlights one of the ways in which developments and policies in some countries may significantly affect developments in other countries in the region.

In sum, estimates of these four indicators suggest some of the principal capabilities and constraints that will condition the future Asian security environment. Toward the end of the report, we will draw from the estimates several implications and conclusions bearing on the future security environment in Asia.

Our estimates build on, update, and expand upon previous RAND work that applied a similar methodology to estimating these same key indicators for many of the same countries.[1] The previous estimates extended from 1950 to 2010, while our new estimates start from 1994, drawing from and, in some instances (e.g., for China and Korea), substantially modifying the previous estimates. These modifications include several changes in basic assumptions underlying the calculations: For example, the previous trend estimates covered South Korea alone, the present estimates cover a unified South and North Korea; the previous estimates proceeded from a single scenario for China's development, the present estimates adopt two dif-

---

[1]See Wolf et al, 1989. See also Hildebrandt, unpublished.

fering scenarios; the previous estimates used purchasing-power-parity (ppp) dollar conversion rates from the early 1980s, while the present estimates use more recent ppp conversion rates.

The calculations reported here cover estimates of these four indicators for the United States, China, Japan, Korea, Taiwan, and India.[2] In reporting our results, we faced a choice between focusing successively on each country, or instead on each of the four functional categories—GDP, per-capita GDP, military spending, and military capital—for the six countries. We have chosen the second option on the premise that comparisons among the countries would enhance the value of the results, and these comparisons are highlighted in each of the four categories. However, the appendix to the report adopts the first option, focusing instead on each country as the unit of analysis and elaborating the data, assumptions, judgments, and detailed calculations made for each country.

The framework for these estimates ignores the possibility of such major exogenous events as serious military conflicts, protracted and severe protectionism, or an oil crisis, as well as the potential effects of trends in one country (e.g., China) on the policies and trends in others. For these and other reasons elaborated in the report, the estimates should be interpreted and used with caution.

Chapter Two summarizes our principal empirical estimates for GDP, per-capita GDP, military spending, and military capital stocks, respectively. Chapter Three then suggests some general inferences and conclusions from the empirical work with respect to its bearing on the future security environment. The report's appendix describes the methodology followed in the empirical work, the reasons for using ppp conversion rates in the calculations, and the data sources, key assumptions, and judgments affecting the estimates for each country. In brief, the appendix explains the aggregate Cobb-Douglas-Solow (CDS) production function and the basis for its use in the calculations; the hierarchic linking of the CDS results to successive estimation of per-capita GDP, military spending, and

---

[2]Selection of these countries was principally based on their relevance in other related and continuing work in the Department of Defense on the future security environment. Subsequent work will report on the corresponding estimates for Russia, Germany, and Indonesia.

military capital; and the reasons for certain key assumptions (e.g., concerning rates of expected productivity growth in each country) that figure prominently in the calculations.

Chapter Two

PRINCIPAL RESULTS

Unless otherwise indicated, all of the calculations made in this work and cited below are presented in 1994 dollars calculated on the basis of purchasing power parity (ppp) exchange rates between the national currencies of the countries concerned and the U.S. dollar, as estimated in the Penn World Tables.[1] These exchange rates show the relative capacity of each country's currency to buy the goods and services produced in that country if these goods and services are valued at prices corresponding to those prevailing in the United States.

There are advantages and disadvantages in using ppp exchange rates for purposes of international comparisons, as there are advantages and disadvantages in using nominal exchange rates for making such comparisons. These points are discussed in the appendix, which deals with methodology. The work summarized in this report is based on the judgment that ppp exchange rates are preferable for making baseline estimates of the relative magnitudes of the aggregate indicators with which we are concerned. Of course, use of nominal exchange rates would drastically—and, in our judgment, misleadingly—alter our results: for example, raising substantially the level of Japan's GDP and severely reducing that of China.

All the GDP growth rates referred to below have been *derived from* the model and methodology discussed in the appendix.

---

[1] Summers and Heston, 1991. In some cases, e.g., China, the Mark 5 estimates have been updated by later Penn World Table estimates.

GROSS DOMESTIC PRODUCT

According to our baseline calculations, the U.S. GDP is currently approximately $6.7 trillion dollars. The GDP of Japan ($2.6 trillion) is about 40 percent as large as that of the United States, while China's current GDP is appreciably larger than that of Japan, and nearly three-quarters the size of the U.S. GDP.

Over the next two decades to 2015, the ratio between the GDPs of the Japanese and U.S. economies changes only slightly, from 39 percent to 42 percent, because Japan's average annual growth rate over this period is estimated at 2.6 percent versus 2.2 percent for the United States.

In calculating China's GDP, we use two different scenarios: (1) a "stable-growth" scenario, in which capital formation and factor productivity are higher (although still well below their actual levels in recent years), resulting in an average annual growth rate of 4.9 percent over the 1994–2015 period, and (2) a "disrupted-growth" scenario, in which turmoil and disruption are assumed to accompany a possible leadership succession crisis, and in which some degree of regional fragmentation ensues. The result is to lower the rate of capital formation and factor productivity growth, yielding an average annual GDP growth of 3 percent over the period. The two scenarios suggest, without exhausting, the numerous uncertainties surrounding China's future and our estimates of its economic and military trends. These uncertainties warrant particular caution in interpreting the China estimates and making inferences from them.

In both of the China scenarios, the ppp exchange rates that we use are at the high end of rates used by others—for example, the ppp rates used in some World Bank calculations are about half the rates we use. While recognizing the imprecision of all these rates, the reasons that seem to us to justify the ones used in this study are explained in some detail in the appendix.

In the disrupted-growth scenario, China's GDP reaches a level of $9 trillion by 2015, which is approximately 85 percent of that of the United States at that time ($10.7 trillion). In the stable-growth scenario, China's GDP by 2015 reaches a level of $13.6 trillion—approximately 27 percent above that of the United States in that year.

GDP estimates for Korea are calculated according to three different scenarios, each involving reunification of the peninsula in 1995, an arbitrary and admittedly unrealistic assumption that is made to permit focusing on the post-reunification growth trajectories in the three cases. If reunification occurs at a (more realistic) later date, we expect that the growth trajectories associated with the three differing scenarios will still ensue, even though their starting point would differ from that posited in our calculations. The three scenarios proceed from differing assumptions about the process through which reunification is accomplished: (1) a "soft-landing" scenario, which implies a peaceful, stable, and mutually accommodating unification process, in which nondistorting macroeconomic policies are pursued; (2) reunification accomplished along lines of the German experience in 1990, in which macroeconomic policies introduced distortions in the relationships between wages, productivity, and prices; and (3) reunification by war, followed by benign, nondistorting economic policies. In the second scenario, economic integration between the South and the North occurs through policies that raise wages in the North at a faster pace than the market will bear, resulting in transitional unemployment and higher costs imposed on the South.

In the third scenario, the war results in a South Korean victory, with half of the civil as well as military capital destroyed in both South and North Korea. As a result, GDP in this scenario declines in 1996 by 17 percent, compared with that in the soft-landing scenario. By 2005, the growth path of the war scenario converges with that of the other two scenarios.[2] These three scenarios, and especially the 1995 time period in which reunification is assumed to occur, are heuristic artifacts intended to illustrate some of the relevant possibilities. Although the trajectories of GDP growth that unfold in the three scenarios are somewhat different from one another, by 2015 the *levels* of GDP in a unified Korea are nearly identical in the three scenarios. Starting from the 1994 level of Korea's GDP of 404 billion in 1994 dollars, representing about 16 percent of Japan's current GDP, a re-

---

[2]By way of comparison, World War II resulted in GDP reductions in Germany and Japan of about 12 percent and 25 percent, respectively. After the war, convergence with prewar growth trends occurred in about 10 years in Germany and 15 years in Japan. See Gordon, 1993.

unified Korea's GDP in all three scenarios reaches by 2015 approximately $2 trillion, about 45 percent of the Japanese GDP in that year.

Taiwan's GDP, starting just below $300 billion in 1994, rises by 2015 to approximately $861 billion, at which time its GDP represents nearly 10 percent of China's GDP in the disrupted-growth scenario, but only 6 percent of China's GDP in the stable-growth scenario.

India's economy maintains a steady and high growth rate, averaging 5.5 percent annually over the next two decades, rising from a level of $1.2 trillion in 1994 to $3.7 trillion in 2015, representing an increase in relative size from about 46 percent of the GDP of Japan in 1994 to approximately 82 percent by 2015. These estimates are predicated on the assumption that India continues its progress with economic liberalization and a relatively reduced state sector.

The GDP forecasts for the six countries and the several scenarios are summarized in Table 1 and Figure 1.

Table 1

Gross Domestic (National) Products of Selected Countries 1994–2015

Country/Year	1994	2000	2006	2015	Average Annual Growth Rates,[a]
	(in billions of ppp 1994 dollars)				1994–2015 (%)
United States	6,704	7,791	8,852	10,673	2.2
Japan	2,593	3,114	3,642	4,509	2.6
China (1) stable-growth	4,950	6,602	8,808	13,569	4.9
China (2) disrupted-growth	4,859	5,802	6,928	9,039	3.0
Korea (1) soft-landing reunification	409	787	1,221	2,024	7.9
Korea (2) German-case reunification	409	776	1,216	2,021	7.9
Korea (3) war reunification	409	726	1,180	2,001	7.3
Taiwan	285	370	541	861	5.4
India	1,193	1,675	2,324	3,693	5.5

[a]These rates have been averaged over the entire period from 1994 through 2015. The estimated rates vary for different intervals over the 21-year period.

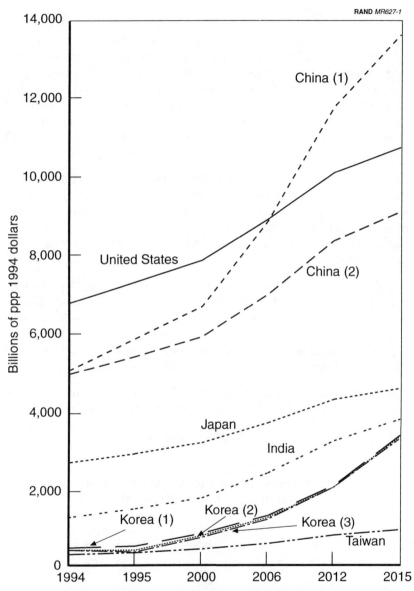

RAND *MR627-1*

NOTE: For the relatively small differences among the three Korean contingencies, see Table 1.

Figure 1—Gross Domestic (National) Products of Selected Countries, 1994–2015

PER-CAPITA GDP

Our estimates for per-capita GDP show, not surprisingly, a strikingly different picture of the relative parities among the six countries from that conveyed by the aggregate GDP figures. Currently, Japan's per-capita GDP is about 20 percent below that of the United States ($21 thousand versus $26 thousand). By 2015, the per-capita GDPs of the two countries are approximately equal. Also by that date, the per-capita GDPs of Korea and Taiwan reach the same level (about $35 thousand) as those attained by the United States and Japan.

China's per-capita GDP, about $4,000 in 1994, is about 20 percent of the per-capita GDP of Japan. By 2015, its per-capita GDP reaches about $10 thousand in the stable-growth scenario, nearly 30 percent of that of Japan. In the disrupted-growth scenario, China's per-capita GDP in 2015 remains about one-fifth of the level in Japan—the same proportion as in 1994.

India's per-capita GDP in 2015 reaches a level of about 70 percent of that of China's in 1994. The ratio between the Indian and Chinese per-capita GDPs in 2015 is 30 percent in China's stable-growth scenario, and 45 percent in its disrupted-growth scenario. The per-capita GDP figures are based on population estimates for 1994 and the assumed population growth rates shown in Table 2.

The per-capita GDP figures shown in Table 3 are derived from the GDP estimates in Tables 1 and the population estimates in Table 2.

The Table 3 data are displayed graphically in Figure 2.

Table 2

1994 Populations and 1994–2015 Population Growth Rates of Selected Countries

Country	1994 Population (millions)	Growth Rate 1994–2015 (%/yr.)
United States	261	.98
Japan	125	.25
China	1,193	.79
Korea	68	1.45
Taiwan	21	.95
India	899	1.76

Table 3

**Per-Capita GDPs of the United States and Selected Countries
(in thousands of ppp 1994 dollars)**

Country	1994	2000	2006	2015
United States	25.7	28.2	30.3	33.2
Japan	20.7	24.4	28.3	34.3
China (1)	4.2	5.3	6.7	9.6
China (2)	4.1	4.6	5.3	6.4
Korea	6.0	10.6	15.0	21.7
Taiwan	13.6	16.6	23.0	33.6
India	1.3	1.7	2.1	2.9

MILITARY SPENDING

The military spending estimates for the six countries are recursively derived from the GDP figures for each country. The derivation applies a parameter, γ, representing the expected share of GDP devoted to military spending in each country. This parameter is estimated from recent experience in each country and combined with judgments about expected changes in its value in the next two decades.[3]

For the United States, the value of γ is based on the *Economic Report of the President, 1994*, which anticipates a reduction in the military spending share of GDP from 4 percent to 3 percent by 1998, a share we assume will continue through 2015.

For Japan, two different cases are assumed. In one case, the military spending share of GDP is set at 1 percent, which has been Japan's standard budgetary practice in recent years. In the second case, the share is set at 3 percent to allow for circumstances in which Japan might increase its military allocations in response to, or anticipation of, security developments in the region. Implicitly, we assume that, if Japan were to raise its military spending, the increases would be realized at the expense of consumption rather than investment; hence, GDP growth would not be affected.

---

[3]For further discussion of the parameter values assumed for each country, see the appendix.

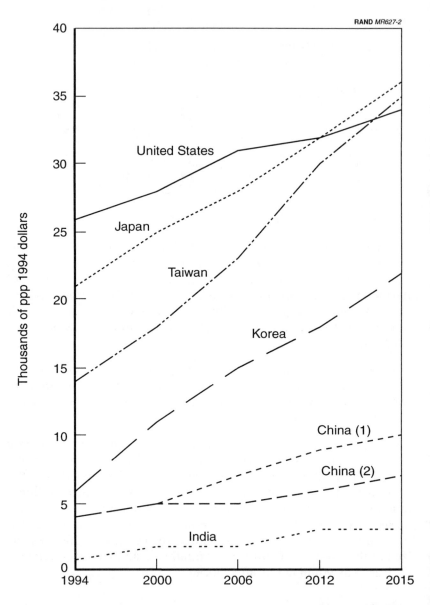

Figure 2—Per-Capita GDPs of the United States and Selected Countries

For China, the military spending share ranges between 3 percent and 3.5 percent in the stable-growth scenario, and remains at 3 percent in the disrupted-growth case.[4] This military spending share reflects our judgment that several additions to the official figures are warranted: first, added funding that is provided to the military but is included in other ministerial budgets than that of the military; second, part of the proceeds from foreign military sales redound to the military establishment; and third, net revenues from civilian commercial sales by industries controlled by the defense establishment also accrue in part to the military establishment.

On these assumptions, China's military spending begins to exceed that of the United States early in the first decade of the 21st century in China's stable-growth scenario, while remaining well below that of the United States in the disrupted-growth scenario.

Japan's military spending remains substantially below that of the United States, for both the 3 percent and 1 percent military spending scenarios.

For Taiwan, the military spending share is set at 5 percent of GDP, for Korea at 4 percent, and for India between 3.5 percent and 4 percent over the 1994–2015 period.

Taiwan's military spending, currently about 7 percent of that of China, rises slightly relative to that of China by 2015.

Korea's military spending, which is currently somewhat below that of Japan ($21 billion versus $26 billion for Japan), exceeds Japan's military spending by the year 2000 and thereafter in the scenario in which Japan's military spending share is 1 percent. Korea's military spending remains below that of Japan if Japan's military spending share increases to 3 percent of its GDP. India's military spending, about $42 billion in 1994, reaches a regionally significant scale of $148 billion by 2015, which represents 41 percent of China's military spending level in China's disrupted-growth scenario, and about 23 percent of China's higher military spending level in the stable-growth scenario.

---

[4]These shares are considerably higher (by a factor of 2) than China's official estimates. The reasons for our estimates are explained more fully in the appendix.

The military spending forecasts are summarized in Table 4 and Figure 3.

MILITARY CAPITAL STOCKS

As noted earlier, the military capital estimates presented here have been built up recursively, starting with pre-1994 estimates contained in our prior work.[5] The pre-1994 estimates have been adjusted in several ways: to reflect the later Penn World Table ppp figures,[6] to shift the base year from 1986 to 1994, to add the capital stock increments from 1994 based on the specified military procurement and construction share of annual military spending, and to allow for depreciation of the previously accumulated capital stock.

The new military capital stock estimates are derived by applying a parameter, π, to the annual military spending estimates, represent-

Table 4

Military Spending Estimates
(in billions of ppp 1994 dollars)

Country	1994	2000	2006	2015
United States	290	235	267	322
Japan (1)	26	31	36	45
Japan (2)	78[a]	93	109	135
China (1)	149	215	308	475
China (2)	149	174	208	271
Korea (1)	20	32	49	81
Korea (2)	20	31	49	81
Korea (3)	20	29	49	80
Taiwan	14	20	27	43
India	42	67	93	148

[a]The $78 billion figure is what military spending would have been if 3 percent of the Japanese GDP had been devoted to defense, rather than 1 percent.

---

[5]See Wolf et al., 1989, especially pp. 32–34. In this study, military capital estimates were made for the period from 1950 to 1985, expressed in 1986 dollars.

[6]Summers and Heston, 1991.

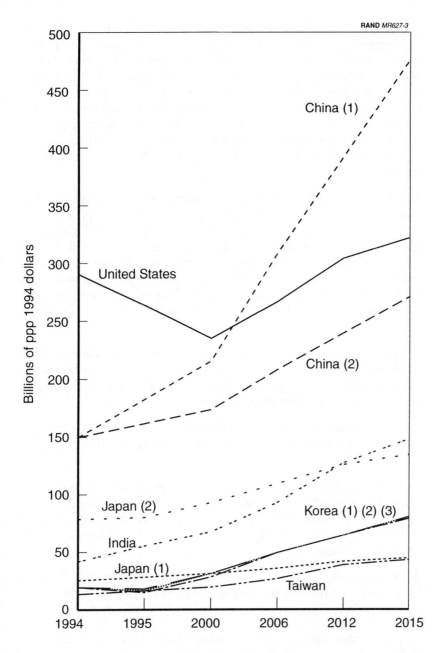

Figure 3—Military Spending Estimates

ing the share of military spending devoted to procurement of military equipment and construction, minus an annual depreciation rate, δ, applied to the previously accumulated capital stock figures. The respective values of π (the military capital share of military spending) and δ (the depreciation rate) are based on recent experience combined with assumptions and judgments about the corresponding values in the future.[7] The values for the capital share, π, vary between 23 percent and 30 percent for the six countries, and their respective annual depreciation rates, δ, vary between 3.5 percent and 6 percent.

The fact that some weapons are imported, rather than domestically produced, introduces another source of imprecision in the military capital stock estimates. The magnitude and direction of this imprecision depends on several complex factors that are not addressed in this study: for example, the gap between nominal and real (i.e., ppp) exchange rates, the extent to which weapons imports are purchased with foreign exchange earned from weapons exports, whether weapons imports are funded by "off-budget" appropriations, and so on.

For the United States, the value of military capital falls over the 1994–2015 period, because additions to U.S. military capital stocks, through procurement and construction, are less than the depreciation of previously accumulated stocks.

Consequently, the military capital stock of $1.1 trillion in 1994 is estimated to fall to about $840 billion by 2015, rising slightly from its nadir in 2011.

Japan's military capital stock rises from 9 percent of that of the United States in 1994 to nearly 20 percent in 2015 in Japan's 1 percent military spending scenario, and to just over half the size of the U.S. military capital stock by 2015 in Japan's 3 percent military spending scenario.

Korea's military capital in 2015 remains about 80 percent of Japan's in the latter's 1 percent military spending scenario, while decreasing

---

[7]For further discussion of the parameter values for π and δ, see the appendix to this report.

sharply in relative terms if Japan raises its military spending to 3 percent of GDP.

China's military capital becomes hugely dominant in the Asia-Pacific region, reaching about 55 percent of the U.S. level in 2015, in China's stable-growth scenario ($456 billion for China compared with $844 billion for the United States in that year). In the disrupted-growth scenario, China's military capital is about 37 percent of that of the United States in 2015.

Taiwan's military capital increases modestly relative to that of China. India's military capital rises appreciably relative to that of China, reaching by 2015 a level of about 77 percent of China's military capital in the stable-growth scenario, and slightly exceeding that of China's in the disrupted-growth scenario ($333 billion military capital for India in 2015 compared with $313 billion for China).

The military capital stock figures are summarized in Table 5 and Figure 4.

Table 5

**Military Capital Stocks of the United States and Selected Countries
(in billions of ppp 1994 dollars)**

Country	1994	2000	2006	2015
United States	1,103	961	858	844
Japan (1)	101	106	127	163
Japan (2)	101	199	293	433
China (1)	202	232	291	456
China (2)	202	219	249	313
Korea (1)	72	68	83	129
Korea (2)	72	67	82	128
Korea (3)	72	43	66	119
Taiwan	30	46	63	101
India	79	126	192	333

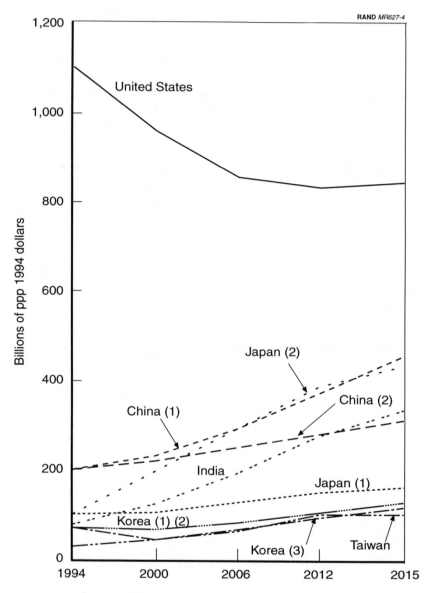

Figure 4—Military Capital Stocks of the United States
and Selected Countries

Chapter Three

CONCLUDING OBSERVATIONS

In words that have been variously attributed to Yogi Berra and Sam Goldwyn, "It is dangerous to make predictions, especially about the future!" The abundant cautions that should be attached to all economic forecasts are familiar enough. They are especially pertinent to the work summarized in this report, as they were to the earlier forecasts to which we have previously referred.[1]

The uncertainties surrounding our forecasts result from many sources: uncertainties traceable directly to the model, uncertainties relating to our estimates and judgments about key parameters in the models, uncertainties deriving from the individual country data and their comparability across countries, uncertainties resulting from possible changes that might ensue in the behavior of countries and their decisionmakers if some of the forecasted trends actually unfold, and uncertainties relating to the possible occurrence of disruptive, exogenous events. Paradoxically, some of the forecasts—especially for the later years—might turn out to be wrong because other forecasts—especially for the earlier years—were accurate. For example, if China's military capital were to reach the large and perhaps alarming scale of the estimates we have made, military spending and procurement by other countries including (the United States) might change substantially, thereby contradicting our forecasts. Alterna-

---

[1]In the earlier RAND forecasts (reported in Wolf et al., 1989), those that erred most seriously dealt with the then-Soviet Union and West Germany. The dissolution of the Soviet Union in 1991 and the reunification of East and West Germany were "state-of-the-world" changes that we did not foresee. Similarly, other major contextual changes that we have not allowed for might invalidate our present estimates.

tively, China's anticipation of such a response might exercise downward pressure on its own military allocations, thereby making the China forecasts faulty. In this sense, our forecasts might be "self-preventing," rather than "self-fulfilling."

Still further uncertainties arise as to how these forecasts would indeed affect the future security environment—even if the forecasts themselves turned out to be accurate—or be affected by that environment if, for example, serious internal or international military conflicts occurred in the region. As noted earlier, many other factors—political, social, ethnic, technological, historical—besides the particular economic and military trends we have estimated, will influence this environment.

Moreover, other factors besides those we have considered will influence the relative economic standing and power of the specific countries with which we have dealt: for example, their respective exports and imports, capital flows, resource allocations for research and development, and their international holdings of assets and liabilities. And, of course, other indicators besides military spending and military capital stocks will affect the strictly military reach and power of these countries: notably, the size of their forces; their forces' training, morale, and leadership; their command and control; their logistics and other infrastructural capabilities; and the regional alliances or adversarial circumstances they confront. We have not analyzed the extent to which these other ingredients of military capabilities would be encompassed by the 70–75 percent noncapital shares of total military spending, or how these noncapital shares might be employed to enhance military effectiveness through changes in technology, organization, and operations in the military establishments of these countries.

While acknowledging the numerous grounds for caution in applying and interpreting our estimates, several inferences can be drawn from them that bear on the future security environment in Asia:

1. The long-term trends projected here probably foreshadow a tremendous growth, over the next two decades, of both economic

and military power in the Asian region relative to that in the rest of the world.[2]

2. Within the Asian region, the parities among the Asian countries will change significantly, and the disparities among them will grow, both in economic and military terms. China's aggregate economic as well as military capabilities will grow significantly relative to most of the other countries in the region, except India. Yet, the economic well-being of China's populace (as crudely measured by per-capita GDP) will remain substantially below that of most other countries in the region.

3. Korea's economic capabilities are likely to grow relative to those of Japan, as will its relative military strength, unless Japan increases its military efforts.

4. India is likely to become a more significant actor in the region, in both economic and military terms, and will probably increase in both dimensions relative to China.

5. Economically and militarily, the United States will remain prominent throughout the region, although its relative scale and scope will diminish.

6. Finally, it remains to be seen whether and how these changes in the relative scale and influence of the national actors in the region will be modified or channeled by powerful, contemporaneous *transnational* trends—for example, trends toward international security alliances, transnational business alliances, and transnational informational and occupational communication and transactions. These transnational trends have not been considered in the work described here.

---

[2]Of course, the analysis reported here does not address the "rest of the world"; so the judgment expressed above concerning *relative* growth is impressionistically based on other studies and sources. Compare *OECD World Economic Outlook*, 1995.

METHODS AND DATA SOURCES

This appendix describes the methodology and data sources used in estimating economic and military trends over the 1994–2015 period for the United States, China, Japan, Korea, Taiwan, and India. The discussion below begins by addressing the general method we have applied in all of these countries, apart from adjustments made for specific countries because of data limitations or other particular circumstances pertaining to those countries. Further explanation of these adjustments, as well as of the specific data sources used for each country, are presented in the later sections of the appendix, which deal with the individual countries. In each country section, we include tables covering the GDP, per-capita GDP, military spending, and military capital estimates for that country. Our estimates for China are probably the most controversial among the six countries covered here; hence, the tables, discussion, and explanation of the China estimates are considerably more extensive and detailed than those for any other country.

METHODOLOGY

The forecasts of economic and military trends presented in this report are based on a hierarchically linked model in which (1) GDP (or gross national product—GNP[1]) is estimated from a CDS production

---

[1]In most cases, the estimates we present are for GDP. In the case of India, the estimates are for GNP because the country data from which the estimates were made used GNP rather than GDP as a starting point. The accounting relation between GDP and GNP is defined as: GDP = GNP – net factor income from abroad.

function, (2) per-capita GDP is calculated using demographic data for each country in combination with our GDP estimates, (3) military spending is derived as a specified (sometimes varying) proportion of GDP, and (4) military capital stocks are estimated as a specified (sometimes varying) proportion of military spending *minus* depreciation of the previously accumulated military capital stock.

Use of the CDS model is based on its commendable transparency, convenience for calculation purposes, and its more modest and tractable data requirements compared, say, with input-output models, translog production functions, or time-series regressions. The method used to derive military spending and military capital estimates was selected for similar reasons of tractability, simplicity, and transparency.

The model summarized below was used for each country, together with adjustments and elaboration to allow for data problems or other country-specific circumstances.

$$Q = (e^{\tau t}) \cdot L^{\alpha} \cdot K^{(1-\alpha)} \tag{1}$$

$$MS_t = \gamma GDP \tag{2}$$

$$MK_t = \pi MS_t + MK_{t-1}(1 - \partial) \tag{3}$$

In Eq. (1):

Q =   GDP

τ =   rate of technological change (total factor productivity)

t =   years covered in the projections beginning with 1994

α =   labor share in GDP

L =   labor input in each year

K =   capital input in each year.

In Eq. (2):

MS_t =   military spending in year t,

γ =   proportion of GDP devoted to military spending.

In Eq. (3):

MK_t =   military capital stock in year t

π =   proportion of military spending devoted to procurement of equipment and construction

∂ =   depreciation rate on the previously accumulated military capital stock.

In Eq. (1), the civil capital inputs (K) and labor inputs (L), and their corresponding growth rates, were estimated for each country, as described in the individual country sections of this appendix. The capital input, K, for each year was calculated by adding each year's capital formation to the previous year's civil capital stock and subtracting depreciation on the previous civil capital stock.[2] Note that this depreciation rate on the civil capital stock is not necessarily the same as the depreciation rate on the military capital stock.

Eq. (1) can be expressed in a form that is useful for our forecasts by taking the logarithmic derivatives of the variables with respect to time. The result is Eq. (1a):

$$\dot{Q}/Q = \tau + \alpha\left(\dot{L}/L\right) + \left(1 - \alpha\right)\left(\dot{K}/K\right) \qquad \text{(1a)}$$

Eq. (1a) stipulates that the rate of growth in GDP is equal to the annual growth of total factor productivity (technological progress) τ, plus the rate of growth in employment multiplied by the share of labor income in GDP (α), plus the rate of growth in the capital stock multiplied by the share of capital income in GDP, $(1 - \alpha)$. The rate of growth in total factor productivity in each country in recent years can

---

[2]The initial year 1994 capital stock figures are derived from the Penn World Table data (see Summers and Heston, 1991, and from the prior estimates in Wolf et al., 1989).

be estimated from the known values of the other variables in Eq. (1a): These known values are obtained from the specific data sources cited for each country in the later sections of this appendix.

Similarly, the labor and capital income shares, (α) and $(1 - \alpha)$, respectively, are based on the respective data and experience of each country.

Similarly, the estimates of the parameter γ, representing the share of GDP devoted to military spending, are calculated from each country's average share in recent years, combined with explicit judgments by the authors of this report.

Measurement of the military capital stock presents complex and difficult theoretical and empirical problems. Among these difficulties are the following: First, the "services" provided by military equipment are difficult to define and quantify; second, the same piece of equipment can provide varying levels of effective service depending on the type of conflict, terrain, adversaries, allies, training, and morale of the forces, as well as various contingency-specific circumstances. Our methodology measures the value of the military capital stock based on procurement cost. This implicitly assumes that the value of military services provided by a particular piece of equipment or structure, relative to others, averaged over an appropriate set of scenarios, is equal to its procurement cost. This assumption is convenient, but arbitrary and untested.

A further difficulty in measuring military capital relates to the possibility of accelerated obsolescence depending on the technology embodied in an adversary's military capital and military forces.

Generally, in our analysis, the military capital stocks of the respective countries were calculated using gross constant-price outlays for military procurement and constructions (covering barracks, airfields, communication facilities, and other structures). As with the civilian capital stock estimates referred to earlier, military capital estimates require that we have a benchmark estimate for at least a single year to enable the entire series to be generated. We have used various methods to establish the initial military capital stock figure, sometimes drawing on the estimates made in our earlier work[3] or adopting other methods described in the individual country sections below. The depreciation rates for the military capital stock are also described in the individual country sections.

It should be noted that our estimates for 1994 through 2015 assume that each country's military spending decisions are independent of those of other countries; i.e., reactive effects were not modeled.

PURCHASING-POWER-PARITY CURRENCY CONVERSION

In general, the trend analyses for each country were initially conducted in constant-price outlays for the respective national currencies. These results were then converted to constant 1994 dollar prices, using the ppp conversion rate reported in the Penn World Tables for 1991 referred to earlier, or to more recent ppp rates from the same authors (Summers and Heston), cited in the corresponding individual country sections. This conversion rate represents the real bilateral exchange rate between each currency and the U.S. dollar, as determined by the relative levels of their respective prices.

Use of the ppp conversion rate raises a question concerning its appropriateness compared with, say, the prevailing nominal bilateral exchange rate between each currency and the dollar, or a moving average of that rate. The ppp rate for each country represents a comparison of prices within specified product or service categories of expenditures, expressed as an average of each category's national prices, relative to the average national prices for the corresponding category in the United States in a specified base year. Hence, the aggregate ppp rate purports to measure what a unit of the corresponding national currency can buy relative to the U.S. dollar if output in the national economy were priced at prevailing U.S. dollar prices.

Economists have generally accepted the proposition that ppp rates and nominal exchange rates differ substantially, as well as systematically, from each other: The ratio between the ppp's of countries' currencies and their nominal exchange rates is an increasing function of their per-capita GDP; i.e., the purchasing power of the dollar

---

[3]See Wolf et al., 1989.

relative to that of a local national currency will be less than the local currency's nominal exchange value in countries with lower per-capita GDPs than that of the United States.[4] Some recent work suggests that, when proper allowance is made for errors-in-variables and lead-and-lag effects, there is a significant relationship between changes in real exchange rates—that is, in relative domestic and foreign prices (for both tradable and nontradable goods)—and changes in nominal exchange rates.[5]

In general, we subscribe to the view that the ppp conversion rates are more appropriate for converting GDP in national currencies to dollars than are prevailing nominal exchange rates. The reason for this view is that ppp rates more accurately reflect the real resource parities among currencies, unaffected by such financial transactions as short-term changes in capital movements and expectations that heavily influence nominal exchange rates. However, it can be argued that use of ppp conversion rates for intercountry comparisons exaggerates the relative magnitudes of poorer economies (e.g., China's), because of the inflated values that this accords to services in these economies.[6] While the argument has some merit, it ignores one of the striking findings of the Summers and Heston work: namely, that "there is almost a flat relationship between real service shares and [per-capita] income . . . quite contrary to the conventional wisdom" (Summers and Heston, 1991, p. 339).

Moreover, in some cases, such as the measurement of military capital stocks, the appropriate rate for comparative cross-sectional analysis could differ from *both* the exchange rate and the ppp conversion rate because some military capital is procured at costs reflecting domestic prices (e.g., indigenously manufactured equipment, construction, etc.), while other military capital is procured at prevailing foreign exchange rates. A further complication arises because some military capital may be procured at prices that involve commodity "offsets" and associated quid-pro-quo transactions, which further obscures the actual conversion rate implicit in the acquisition.

---

[4]See Summers and Heston, 1991, p. 335.

[5]See Apte et al., 1994.

[6]China's ppp conversion rate has been about six times greater than its nominal exchange rate, while Japan's ppp rate is about 40–50 percent *below* its nominal rate.

As previously noted, interpretation of the results that we report should proceed with caution because of the currency conversion process we have followed, the numerous problems of data reliability and comparability described below, and the wide range of uncertainty about political and security trends and relationships in the Asia-Pacific region.

COUNTRY DATA SOURCES AND METHODS

United States

Data Sources. Data for the U.S. GDP and its components, and for U.S. employment, come from the *Economic Report of the President, 1994.* The 1991 version of this document has some earlier data that are not in the 1994 version. Defense spending data are disaggregated into equipment and structures purchases and other components that are found in U.S. Department of Commerce, 1988, and various issues of the *Survey of Current Business* (U.S. Department of Commerce, various years). Data on both military and civilian capital stocks are in the *Survey of Current Business* (U.S. Department of Commerce, January 1992 and September 1993).

The population data and projection are from U.S. Department of Commerce, 1993.

Estimation. The increase of the GDP deflator from 1993 to 1994 is assumed to be the same as in the prior year: 2.6 percent. Projections after that time are in constant 1994 dollars.

In the U.S. projections, the labor share of GDP is assumed to be 0.65, which was the 1959–1993 average. (Labor's income share is estimated from the previous data sources as "compensation of employees" divided by [GDP minus "direct business taxes"]).

This is equivalent to assuming that the relative incidence of indirect business taxes on capital and labor is the same as their proportion in total GDP. All of proprietor and partnership income are allocated to capital.

Employment is assumed to increase between 1994 and 2000 by 1.6 percent annually, which is the same rate shown in the *Economic*

Report of the President, 1994. After 2000, employment is assumed to increase 1 percent per year, reflecting demographic changes in the proportion of new entrants to the labor force. Total factor productivity (the parameter τ in Eq. (1) of the model) is assumed to grow by 0.65 percent per year from 1994 to 2015, which is the 1959–1993 average.

Fixed private investment as a percentage of GDP is assumed to be 15.7, the 1959–1993 average. Depreciation of the private fixed capital stock is assumed to be 6 percent annually, which was the 1983–1993 average. This depreciation rate has been increasing in recent years, reflecting shorter-lived equipment stocks, such as computers.

Defense spending is assumed to equal the percentage of GDP projected in the *Economic Report of the President, 1994.* From 1994 to 1999, this document shows the military spending share (the parameter γ in Eq. (2) of the model), falling to 3 percent in 1999. It is projected to stay at 3 percent through 2015.

The share of equipment purchases in defense spending (the parameter π in Eq. (3)) is projected to fall from the 1993 level of 26 percent by 1 percentage point per year to 20 percent in 1999, and to stay at 20 percent thereafter. This estimate is consistent with the lower proportions of equipment purchases that occurred during the relatively low defense spending levels in the 1970s. The equipment share rose in the 1980s. Consideration of the importance of avoiding a "hollow" force lead us to project a reduction in the equipment share to the proportions of the 1970s. The share of construction purchases in defense spending is projected to rise from its 1993 level of 1.9 percent to a 2002 level of 2.3 percent, and to remain at that level, which was the construction share in the 1972–1993 average. Thus, the military capital share (the parameter π in Eq. (3) of the model), which includes both procurement of equipment and construction, varies between 28 percent and 22.3 percent of military spending over the 1994–2015 period.

The depreciation rate of military equipment, (∂ in Eq. (3)) is projected to be 10 percent from 1994 through 2015, which is the 1972–1993 average. The depreciation rate of military construction is projected to be 3 percent over the period covered by our estimates, which is the 1982–1993 average. This shorter period was chosen to reflect a sharp rise in the rate of depreciation in the military construction part of the capital stock between 1972 and 1993.

Our estimates show a real rate of growth of the GDP of 2.5 percent per year between 1994 and the end of the century, with this rate projected to fall to slightly above 2 percent in the early 21st century. This fall is due to lower labor-force growth, which in turn results from lower projected population growth.

Also in our calculations, by 2000, real defense spending is 25 percent lower than its 1993 level, and 37 percent below the 1987 peak. This is because the share of defense in GDP falls, according to the administration's plan, to just about 3 percent of GDP in the year 2000. Defense spending is assumed to stabilize at 3 percent of GDP after 2000, so the real volume of military spending begins to rise thereafter. The military capital stock, which peaked in 1993, falls 1.5 percent per year between 1993 and 2011, when it bottoms out. This is because the military equipment and construction components of military spending are not sufficient to keep up with the scrapping of older military equipment, also reflected in declining force structure and weapon stocks in the military.

Table A.1 summarizes the principal trend results for the United States.

Table A.1

United States: Trend Estimates

	1994	2000	2006	2015	
GDP (billions of ppp 1994 $)	$6,704	$7,791	$8,852	$10,673	
Average annual growth rate[a] (%)		2.5%	2.2%	2.1%	$\left(\bar{r} = 2.2\%\right)$
GDP per capita (thousands of ppp 1994 $)	$25.7	$28.2	$30.5	$34.1	
Military spending (billions of ppp 1994 $)	$290	$235	$267	$322	$\left(4\% > \gamma \geq 3\%\right)$
Military capital (billions of ppp 1994 $)	$1,103	$961	$858	$844	$\left(23\% < \pi < 28\%\right)$

[a]Total factor productivity growth rate estimated at 0.65 percent annually. $\bar{r}$ is the average annual GDP growth rate over the 1994–2015 period.

Japan

Data Sources. The principal data source used in our estimates is the *Japan Statistical Yearbook, 1993–1994,* (*JSY*), (*JSY*, 1995). More recent data on Japan's national accounts are published in the *Quarterly Economic Review,* 1994, but also originally issued by the Economic Planning Agency, Tokyo, Japan.

The civilian capital stock figures are based on the 1985 estimates of capital stock per worker contained in the Penn World Tables (see Summers and Heston, 1991), multiplied by the employment figures in *JSY,* 1995.

Employment and population data, and their corresponding growth rates, are drawn from *JSY* and the *U.N. Monthly Bulletin of Statistics,* 1994.

The capital share of GDP is from the *National Accounts Estimates of the OECD,* cited by Hale, 1994.

Estimation. In our earlier calculations (see Wolf et al., 1989), we used a labor share in income (the parameter α in Eq. (1) above) of 0.63. The sources cited in the data discussion above provide a range of labor income shares between 0.69 and 0.68, from 1988 to 1994, corresponding to capital shares, $(1 - \alpha)$, between 0.31 and 0.32. In our estimates, a value of α equal to 0.64 is assumed for the rest of this century, thereafter rising to 0.66 and staying at that level through 2015.

In generating the annual investment additions to the initial 1994 capital stock estimates referred to above, we use the same investment share of GDP that was used in Wolf et al., 1989, namely, 28 percent, from 1994 to the year 2000. Thereafter, we assume that the investment share declines slightly to 27 percent of GDP from 2001 through 2005 and decreases further to 26 percent of GDP in the following years through 2015. These reductions are presumed to reflect slightly rising consumption rates (slightly decreasing savings rates) in Japan due to demographic changes and various other reasons.

The annual growth in employment follows the decreasing trend of recent years and, on that basis, is set at 1.7 percent from 1994 through 2000, 1.5 percent for the next 5 years, and 1.2 percent from

2006 through 2015. These decreases reflect Japan's reduced rate of population growth, smaller additions to the labor force, and the aging of Japan's population.

Calculation of the rate of growth in total factor productivity (the parameter τ in Eq. (1) above) is derived as a residual from the actual data for GDP and for capital and labor inputs, in the period from 1987 through 1993. This residual is calculated as the difference between the rate of growth in Japanese GDP in constant prices *minus* the rate of growth in the capital stock (K) and the rate of growth in employment (L), with the latter two terms weighted by their respective income shares $(1 - \alpha)$ and α.

The calculated value for the rate of total factor productivity growth (π) for the period from 1987 through 1993 varies between 0.53 percent and –0.166 percent, depending, respectively, on whether residential construction is included or excluded from the capital stock and from annual capital formation. If residential construction is included, then the rate of growth in the capital stock is slower over the 1987–1993 period; hence, the residual attributed to total factor productivity growth registers as 0.53 percent. If residential construction is excluded, then the rate of growth in the capital stock is more rapid, and total factor productivity growth registers a *negative* rate of –0.166.

In our baseline calculation, we assume that the value of total factor productivity is –0.17 percent in 1994 and increases in annual increments to reach a level of +0.53 percent by 2001, remaining at that level through 2015.

The data for estimating the defense spending share in GDP, γ, and the military investment share of defense spending, π, are derived from Japan Defense Agency, 1993. For the share of military spending in GDP (the parameter γ in Eq. (2)), we use the standard figure of 1 percent, which is approximately the actual share realized in 1991 through 1993. To reflect the possibility of a Japanese decision to increase its military efforts substantially, we also use an alternative military spending share of 3 percent. We implicitly assume that, were such a threefold boost to occur in response to a major policy decision about Japan's need for greater defense preparedness, the requisite financing would principally impinge on domestic consumption, leaving investment and GDP growth unaffected. This assumption has been made in the interest of simplicity, rather than realism.

In projecting the military capital stock for Japan, we use a value of π for the military investment share of military spending of 27 percent, representing 25 percent for purchases of equipment and 2 percent for the costs of military construction. Again, these figures are based on the actual levels reported in Japan Defense Agency, 1993. They do not include host-nation support for U.S. forces and facilities in Japan. This value of π compares with a value of 25 percent used in the projections reported in Wolf et al., 1989; the same annual depreciation rate of 6 percent (the value of ∂ in Eq. (3) of the model) has been used in the new calculations, as well as the prior ones.

Table A.2 summarizes the principal trend results for Japan.

Table A.2

Japan: Trend Estimates

	1994	2000	2006	2015	
GDP (billions of ppp 1994 $)	$2,593	$3,114	$3,642	$4,509	
Average annual growth rate[a] (%)		3.1%	2.6%	2.4%	$\left(\bar{r} = 2.6\%\right)$
GDP as a percentage of U.S. GDP	38.7%	40.0%	41.1%	42.2%	
GDP per capita (thousands of ppp 1994 $)	$20.8	$24.5	$28.2	$33.5	
Military spending (billions of ppp 1994 $) (1)	$26	$31	$36	$45	$\left(\gamma = 1\%\right)$
(2)	$78	$93	$109	$135	$\left(\gamma = 3\%\right)$
Military capital (billion of ppp 1994 $) (1)	$87	$106	$127	$163	$\left(\pi = 27\%\right)$
(2)	$101	$199	$293	$433	
Military capital as a percentage of that of the United States					
(1)	7.9%	11.0%	14.8%	19.3%	
(2)	9.2%	20.7%	34.1%	51.3%	

[a]Total factor productivity is assumed to grow at –0.2 percent/year from 1994 to 2000, and thereafter at ±5/percent/year through 2015. $\bar{r}$ is the average annual GDP growth rate over the 1994–2015 period.

China

Data Sources. Our baseline 1994 GDP estimate is derived from a 1990 GDP estimate by Alan Heston, 1994. This 1990 estimate has been converted to 1994 prices using the implicit price deflator for U.S. GDP in *Economic Indicators, May 1994.* GDP estimates for 1991 through 1993 are based on the 1990 figure and an index of GDP in constant prices for those years given in State Statistical Bureau, 1994a.

There have been many, widely discrepant estimates of China's GDP and per-capita GDP. Those based on nominal exchange rates between the yuan and the dollar—such as in World Bank, 1991—differ by as much as a factor of 10 from other estimates based on real (ppp) exchange rates.[7] There are also substantial discrepancies among the estimates that use ppp rates: For example, the earlier ppp estimates by Kravis et al., 1982; those in Summers and Heston, 1991; and the Field and Taylor estimates (1993) differ from one another by a factor greater than two. Our present estimates—derived from Heston, 1994, which, in turn, updated the earlier Kravis et al. work—are the highest among the numerous ones based on real (ppp) rates.

Admittedly, all the ppp estimates—including our own—suffer from inadequate information about relative prices, matching qualities, and weights. Quality matching is the most onerous of these difficult problems, and, unfortunately, solutions to it are highly arbitrary.

In sum, all the ppp estimates are subject to unknown margins of error, and one cannot say definitively that the margin for any estimate is clearly smaller than for others. Our present estimates use the Summers and Heston, 1991, data for two essential reasons. First, the Summers and Heston, 1991, estimate for China is consistent in methodology with those for other countries in our study. Second, even if it really biased our estimates upwards, as Field and Taylor, 1993, and others would argue, it may well result in an estimate closer to the true figure than others. We know that Kravis et al., 1982, (on whose work Summers and Heston, 1991, is based) took into consideration price subsidies, such as those for housing, in calculating ppp. It is not clear that the others' estimations have done so. This is

---

[7]Compare Ruoen and Xai, 1995.

relevant because the other ppp estimates are based on "official" GNP figures, which are clearly too low. The main reasons that these figures are too low are the underreporting in the service sector and the undervaluation of such services as housing and health care. A recent census of this sector revealed gross underestimates, as a result of which the GDP was revised upwards by significant amounts, as the data in Table A.3 show.

Estimates for the growth of capital and labor inputs and of factor productivity are derived from data for pre-1994 years shown in Li, 1994. The growth of China's capital stock is assumed to be slower in the next two decades than in the recent past because of (1) higher depreciation rates resulting from an increasing share of equipment in total fixed investment (see *China Daily*, 1987), (2) somewhat lower personal savings rates due to international and interregional diffusion of consumption habits (see *The New York Times*, 1992), and (3) reduced government savings resulting from rising environmental protection costs, subsidies to underdeveloped regions of China, and financial losses of state-owned enterprises.

These circumstances are assumed to be more adverse in the disrupted-growth scenario, because its lower GDP growth rate discourages investment and leads to a reduction in the inflow of foreign capital. Growth of the labor input in the stable-growth scenario is the average of the estimate for 1993–2000 (1.5 percent) and that for 2000–2015 (1.04 percent). The former, in turn, is the average of the

Table A.3

Recent Revisions in Services and
GDP (1992 and 1993)

Revisions	1992	1993
Gross value added, services (billions of yuan)	686.3	848.5
Revised	914.0	1,127.7
Percentage (adjusted)	33.2%	32.9%
GDP (billions of yuan)	2,436.3	3,138.0
Revised	2,664.0	3,417.2
Percentage (adjusted)	9.3%	8.9%

SOURCES: State Statistical Bureau, 1994b, p. 32; *Jinrong shibao*, 1994.

actual growth rate from 1990–1993 shown in State Statistical Bureau, 1994c, p. 20, and the projected growth rate for 1992–2000 given in World Bank, 1994a, which in turn is based on the projection for 2000–2010 by Development Research Center, 1994. The labor and capital income shares (α and $(1 - \alpha)$, respectively) are set at 0.6 and 0.4, the same parameter values used in Wolf et al., 1989.

Total factor productivity growth (the parameter τ in Eq. (1)) is derived from Li, 1994, and Junkuang, 1991. These sources show a declining trend in the recent past, which can be explained by the dwindling effect of agricultural reform and several emerging problems, including persistent bottlenecks in energy supply and transportation, inflation, and a relatively inefficient state sector. These factors are likely to continue and perhaps become aggravated in the next two decades by numerous additional difficulties—for example, bottlenecks in the supply of water and certain farm products in addition to those for energy and transportation; the delayed effects of prolonged neglect of investment in human capital in the 1970s and 1980s; continued growth of regional political and economic power, which will enhance the trend of suboptimization at the provincial level; and resistance to further economic reforms by interest groups that oppose them. Offsets to these negative effects will perhaps result from efficiency gains from competition in the growing private sector, expanding foreign trade and technology from abroad, gradual diffusion of economic growth from coastal to interior areas, and closer cooperation between China, Hong Kong, and Taiwan. On balance, we assume that total factor productivity will be positive ($\tau = 1$ percent per year) but slower than in the 1980s in the stable-growth scenario and will stagnate ($\tau = 0$) in the disrupted-growth scenario.

The population figures used in calculating per-capita GDP estimates are based on the average of the two year-end figures for 1990–1993 shown in State Statistical Bureau, 1994c, and the population estimates for 1995–2015, from Development Research Center, 1994.

The average share of defense spending in GDP (γ in Eq. (2)) is placed between 3 percent and 3.5 percent in the stable-growth scenario and held constant at 3 percent in the disrupted-growth scenario. These shares are based on officially reported figures on defense spending given in State Statistical Bureau, 1993 and 1994c, to which we have applied a factor of 2.5 to allow for (1) unreported items that may be carried in nondefense ministerial budgets (e.g., the ministries of energy and nuclear resources, of transportation, of aviation, etc.); (2) net revenues realized by the military from foreign military sales; and (3) net revenues from commercial sales by defense industries that are controlled by the Chinese defense establishment. The ratio of adjusted to official defense spending has been estimated at 3.1 percent for 1991–1992 in International Institute for Strategic Studies (IISS), 1994, as well as in the official totals shown in State Statistical Bureau, 1993, for 1991–1992; at 2.3 percent for 1994 in Bitzinger and Lin, 1994; and at 2.2 percent for 1980–1983, in Defense Intelligence Agency, 1984. Our adjustment factor, 2.5, is the average of these estimates.

The share of military investment in China's defense spending (the parameter π in Eq. (3)) is set at 26 percent, based on the estimated share of equipment purchases (24 percent) and one-half of the share of "other," non–operations and maintenance outlays (4 percent), to allow for expenditures on military construction, shown in Segal and Waller, 1994.

Depreciation of the military capital stock is assumed to be at the relatively high rates of 8 percent in the 1990s and 10 percent in the 2001–2015 period, to allow for accelerated technological obsolescence and replacement. The military capital stock estimate for 1990 is derived from Wolf et al., 1989, adjusted for price changes using the implicit U.S. GDP price deflator, with additions to reflect new military investment in ensuing years and subtractions to allow for depreciation of the accumulated military capital stock.

Estimation. Two scenarios are used for the China projections. The stable-growth scenario assumes that there will be no major political upheavals or social unrest within China or military conflicts with other countries during this period; that economic reform and opening to the outside world continue although at a slower pace; and that no major breakthroughs or innovations will occur. Specifically, we assume in this scenario that there is a smooth political transition to a new leadership that continues Chief of State Deng's reform policies, with continued cooperation between the central and provincial governments in developing an integrated market economy, and that economic liberalization coexists with political totalitarianism—at least for the period covered by these projections. The disrupted-growth scenario is characterized by a leadership succession crisis, which degenerates into a protracted political struggle and ends with the conservatives in power. In this scenario, provinces became more like independent economic fiefdoms, blocking the development of integrated markets. Substantial unemployment and widening gaps in income distribution among regions and groups lead to social unrest and retrogression of many reform measures, which are replaced by direct government controls. In this scenario, the growth of capital and labor inputs is substantially reduced, and factor productivity stagnates. As a result, the GDP annual growth rate for the period 1994–2015 is 4.92 percent in the stable-growth scenario, and 3 percent in the disrupted-growth scenario, as shown in Table A.4. As noted earlier, the two China scenarios suggest, but do not exhaust, the many uncertainties characterizing China's future. Consequently, our estimates should be treated and interpreted with particular caution.

In estimating defense spending and military capital, we use a value between 3.0 percent and 3.5 percent for the parameter γ in Eq. (2), as explained above, 26 percent for the parameter π in Eq. (3), and depreciation rates of 8 percent and 10 percent in the 1990s and the first 15 years of the 21st century, respectively, for reasons previously explained. We assume that the share of defense spending will be

Table A.4

Sources of GDP Growth in China, 1985–1990 and 1994–2015
(in percentage)

	1985–1990	1994–2015 Stable-Growth Scenario	1994–2015 Disrupted-Growth Scenario
Capital input	10.0	8.0	6.0
Labor input	2.7	1.2	1.0
Contributions to GDP growth:			
Capital	4.35	3.2	2.4
Labor	1.56	0.72	0.60
Productivity	1.52	1.0	0
GDP	7.43	4.92	3.0

constant throughout this period because the military has several strong reasons for accelerating military modernization. First, there is still a significant gap between the military technology levels of China and those of the United States and Russia. China's intention to reduce this gap is indicated both by its refusal to halt nuclear tests and by its continued efforts to purchase advanced military technology from Russia and the United States. Second, China's aspiration to become a dominant regional military power requires the development of a blue-ocean navy at least comparable to that of Japan. Third, China evidently seeks to prepare for possible military conflicts in the Spratly Islands, the Taiwan Straits, and Tibet.

To pursue its modernization aims, China's military leaders can probably mobilize additional resources from two sources. First, the People's Liberation Army (PLA) probably will play an important role in the leadership succession process and thus will be in a position to demand more resources from the state budget. Second, China's arms sales and other business enterprises that are run by the PLA can provide additional income to the military. At the same time, the quest for additional military spending is likely to be constrained by priority demands for other purposes such as building infrastructure and other institutions for the market economy and by international pressure to curb the arms trade.

Tables A.5 and A.6 summarize the principal trend results for the stable-growth and disrupted-growth scenarios.

Table A.5

China: Trend Results
(Stable-Growth Scenario)

	1994	2000	2006	2015	
GDP (billions of ppp 1994 $)	$4,950	$6,602	$8,808	$13,569	
Average annual growth rate[a] (%)	4.9%	4.9%	4.9%		$(\bar{r} = 4.9\%)$
GDP as a percentage of U.S. GDP	73.8%	84.7%	99.5%	127.1%	
GDP per capita (thousands of ppp 1994 $)	$4.1	$5.2	$6.7	$9.7	
Military spending (billions of ppp 1994 $)	$149	$215	$308	$475	$(3.25\% < \gamma < 3.50\%)$
Military capital (billions of ppp 1994 $)	$202	$232	$291	$460	$(\pi = 26\%)$
Military capital as percentage of that of the United States	18%	24%	34%	55%	

[a]Total factor productivity is assumed to grow at an annual rate of 1 percent in the stable-growth scenario. $\bar{r}$ is the average annual GDP growth rate in this scenario.

Table A.6

China: Trend Results
(Disrupted-Growth Scenario)

	1994	2000	2006	2015	
GDP (billions of ppp 1994 $)	$4,859	$5,802	$6,928	$9,039	
Average annual growth rate[a] (%)	3.0%	3.0%	3.0%		$(\bar{r} = 3.0\%)$
GDP as a percentage of U.S. GDP	72.5%	74.5%	78.3%	84.7%	
GDP per capita (thousands of ppp 1994 $))	$4.1	$4.6	$5.2	$6.5	
Military spending (billions of ppp 1994 $)	$149	$174	$208	$271	$(\gamma = 3\%)$
Military capital (billions of ppp 1994 $)	$202	$219	$249	$313	$(\pi = 26\%)$
Military capital as a percentage of that of the United States	18%	23%	29%	37%	

[a]Total factor productivity is assumed to grow at an annual rate of 0 percent in the disrupted-growth scenario. $\bar{r}$ is the average annual GDP growth rate in this scenario.

Taiwan

Data Sources. Estimates for Taiwan's GDP are derived from an initial estimate in 1990 presented in Heston, 1994, converted to 1994 prices based on Council for Economic Planning and Development, 1994. Growth of the civilian capital stock is adjusted from the prior growth rates shown from 1970-1980 in Wu, 1983. Growth of the labor input, 1.3 percent for 1990–2000 and 0.7 percent for 2000–2015, is based on the medium projection shown in Manpower Planning Department, 1993 (in "Linear Regression of Manpower Supply on Employment for 1952–1992") and Council for Economic Planning and Development, 1994. The income shares for labor and capital are assumed to be 0.6 and 0.4, respectively, as previously reported in Wolf et al., 1989. Population data and projections are drawn from Manpower Planning Department, 1993.

The growth of total factor productivity has been estimated at 5.6 percent and 3.1 percent, annually, for the 1960–1970 and 1960–1980 periods, respectively (see Wu, 1983). In view of the huge investment in human capital in Taiwan and Taiwan's experience in effectively adapting to external changes, we expect that productivity growth will be lower than in the past but probably will still be at a fairly high rate. This leads us to adopt a value of 2.5 percent per year for the parameter γ in Eq. (1) of the model.

Estimation. In deriving our estimates of Taiwan's GDP growth, we assume that the growth of the capital stock will be 6 percent annually, which is about 25 percent below the 8.1 percent record in the preceding decade. Annual growth of the labor input is expected to be 1.3 percent for 1990–2000 and 0.7 percent for 2000–2015, with the factor shares of 0.4 and 0.6 for capital and labor, respectively. Combining these estimates with the assumed growth of total factor productivity, the resulting annual rate of growth in Taiwan's GDP is 5.7 percent annually for the 1994–2000 period, and 5.3 percent annually for the 2000–2015 period.

Data found in U.S. Arms Control and Disarmament Agency, 1990, and Council for Economic Planning and Development, 1994, suggest that the share of defense spending in GDP (the parameter γ in Eq. (2)) was about 4 percent in 1989–1993. The rising trend toward political independence in Taiwan in recent years has heightened fear of attack from the mainland. Consequently, Taiwan's urge to modernize its military establishment is likely to gain political support from the factions in the government that seek independence. It is also economically and financially feasible for the government to allocate more resources for defense. We therefore assume that the annual share of defense spending of GDP increases slightly to 5 percent.

The calculation of military investment (the parameter π in Eq. (3)) is assumed to be a relatively high 29 percent, reflecting Taiwan's recent and intended emphasis on force modernization.[8] The annual depreciation of the military capital stock is assumed to be 6 percent from 1994–2000, and 7 percent annually thereafter. The increased depreciation rate after 2000 also reflects an increased emphasis on modernization, as well as changes in military technology—both factors imply less "value" accorded to older military capital. Taiwan's total military capital stock is derived from estimates of military investment, depreciation rates, and the initial military capital stock in 1993 given in Wolf et al., 1989, defense spending estimates for 1980–1993 from U.S. Arms Control and Disarmament Agency, 1990, and *Economic Indicators, May 1994*, and defense spending for 1990–1993 from Council for Economic Planning and Development, 1994. The initial military capital stock, in turn, is calculated from the total for 1980 given in Wolf et al., 1989, the defense spending figures for 1980–

---

[8]The 29 percent figure for military investment is similar to that experienced by Korea in the 1975–1983 period. The relevance of the Korean data to Taiwan proceeds from several significant parallels between the two cases:

1. Both countries have faced hostile and militarily strong adversaries only minutes of flying time from their borders.

2. Both faced adversaries with strong Russian-derived military technology and equipment.

3. Both had strong balance-of-payments positions, so they could afford to purchase military equipment from abroad as well as develop their own.

4. Both were at similar levels of economic development, and both had large accumulations of human capital and hence considerable capacity to develop, produce, and use modern weapons.

5. Both had many high-level military and nonmilitary officials involved in decisionmaking about defense resource allocations.

In short, the motivations and capabilities of Taiwan and South Korea have been so similar in defense planning and resource allocations, that South Korea's experience and data are probably the best approximation for estimating the corresponding patterns in Taiwan.

1993 given in U.S. Arms Control and Disarmament Agency, 1990; *Economic Indicators, May 1994;* and Council for Economic Planning and Development, 1994; the share of military investment in defense spending and the depreciation rate are assumed to be 29 percent and 6 percent, respectively.

Table A.7 summarizes the principal trend results for Taiwan.

Table A.7

Taiwan: Trend Results

	1994	2000	2006	2015	
GDP (billions of ppp 1994 $)	$284.7	$396.9	$504.8	$860.8	
Average annual growth rate [a] (%)		5.7%	5.3%	5.3%	$(\bar{r} = 5.4\%)$
GDP as a percentage of China's GDP	5.8%	6.0%	6.1%	6.3%	
GDP per capita (thousands of ppp 1994 $)	$13.5	$17.9	$23.2	$34.9	
Military spending (billions of ppp 1994 $)	$14	$20	$27	$43	$(\gamma = 5\%)$
Military capital (billions of ppp 1994 $)	$30	$46	$63	$101	$(\pi = 29\%)$
Military capital as a percentage of that of China (%)	14.9%	19.8%	21.6%	22.0%	

[a]Total factor productivity growth rate estimated at 2.5 percent annually. $\bar{r}$ is the average annual GDP growth rate over the 1994–2015 period.

Korea

Data Sources. For the general baseline data to size South Korea's GDP, population, and military spending figures, the principal source used is Arms Control and Disarmament Agency, 1994. For the South Korean savings rate, the principal source used is World Bank, 1994b. For the key parameters used in the model, including the depreciation rates, the parameters representing the share of military spending in GDP (γ in Eq. (2)), and the share of military procurement and construction in military spending (π in Eq. (3)), the data used, and assumptions made are taken from Henry, 1986.

Estimation. Three scenarios have been used in the simulations from which our estimates are derived. In all these scenarios, the economies of North and South Korea are assumed to develop separately through 1994 and to be unified in 1995. There are also a series of economic adjustments that are common to the three scenarios, as discussed below. These scenarios are useful to examine the process of economic unification under various assumptions. The nature of the simulations we have conducted and the resulting estimates will not change greatly if unification occurs somewhat later. The change would simply be that the starting date for the major changes arising from an economic merger will be postponed until a later date, but the subsequent growth trajectories will not differ appreciably from those described in the three scenarios below.

A "Soft-Landing" Scenario. This is an optimistic base case in which the merger of the two economies proceeds well, without distortion of economic policies or the destruction of war.

The "German" Scenario. In this case, the government attempts to manage the economic integration through policies aimed at raising wages in the North at a faster pace than the market will bear, resulting in substantial transitional unemployment in the North.

A "War" Scenario. In this case political unification results from a war that the South wins. During the war, half of the civilian capital stock in both the North and South are destroyed, and half the military capital stock is destroyed as well. As in the soft-landing scenario, the subsequent economic policies are assumed to be benign, in contrast to those of the previous post-unification scenario.

The merger of two distinct economies requires the blending or the convergence of the differences between them. The following processes were assumed to occur, for purposes of modeling the transition and the resulting merged economy:

Obsolete Civilian Capital Stock in North Korea. The North Korean economy has been built under nearly autarchic circumstances. When confronted with world prices, some part of the North Korean civilian capital stock will be economically obsolete. This share is assumed to be 25 percent in all three scenarios, and this obsolescence is assumed in each case to occur immediately.

Gains from Trade. As the two economies combine, greater efficiency can be achieved as factor prices converge. North Korean labor is paired with South Korean capital, and the merged economies are assumed to produce more than the sum of the two separately. This convergence is assumed to take place over five years. This assumption is perhaps overoptimistic. The experience in Germany since its reunification in 1990 suggests that convergence there is likely to take at least 10 years. We are assuming, therefore, that the process of reunification, and in particular the accompanying economic policies, will be managed more efficiently so that convergence of factor productivity will be expedited. In the interim, production is a weighted average (with weights changing by 20 percent per year) of the sum of the two economies and the labor and capital inputs of the two economies in combination.

Convergence of Total Factor Productivity. In part because of the socialist system in the North, in part because of the lower technological level there, and in part for a long list of other factors, total factor productivity in the North significantly lags that of the South. It is assumed that the level in the North converges with that in the South over a period of five years—again, perhaps an overoptimistic assumption.

Convergence of Labor Efficiency. The economic system in the North has not provided the populace with the same levels of education and training realized in the South. In addition, the Northern workers are accustomed to working in a nonmarket economic system. Their productivity is likely to be lower than that of workers in the South for several years. Our simulations have assumed a 30 percent deficiency at reunification, with productivity of Northern workers converging with that of Southern workers over a 10-year period.

In making the military spending and military capital estimates, the military share in GDP is assumed to be 4 percent in South Korea and 20 percent in North Korea prior to unification. After unification the military share (γ in Eq. (2)) is set at 4 percent of total GNP. Procurement, including construction, is assumed to be 30 percent of military spending in the South and 50 percent in the North. These shares are somewhat higher than in the other countries. South Korea's high share reflects growth in the budget driven by growth in GNP, and this higher share is supported by historical evidence. In the North an even higher rate is assumed. The North Korean military pays little to their military personnel and has a low operational tempo but has significantly added to its force structure and equipment over the years. After unification, the rate of procurement falls to that of the South for the entire economy.

Both civilian and military capital are assumed to depreciate at an annual rate of 8 percent, which is above that in the United States, because the United States invests relatively more in structures whose depreciation rate is lower.

Total factor productivity growth rates (the parameter τ in Eq. (1)) begin at almost 6 percent in the South and –2 percent in the North. These numbers are based on historical calculations from 1981 through 1991. The rate in the South is assumed to decrease to 3 percent per year by 2015. After unification the productivity level in the North converges with that in the South and then follows the rate maintained by the South.

Savings rates are assumed to be 30 percent in the South and 20 percent in the North, the North again converging toward the 30 percent level in the South after unification.

Table A.8 summarizes the principal trend results for the Korean soft-landing scenario. Results for the other two less favorable scenarios— the "German" and "war" scenarios—are not shown because, while their respective trend trajectories differ from the soft-landing case, the end points, and indeed the final decade of the 1994–2015 period, are closely similar across the three scenarios. As noted earlier, all three scenarios make the admittedly unrealistic assumption that re-unification occurs in 1995.

Table A.8

Korea: Trend Results (Soft-Landing Scenario)

	1994	2000	2006	2015	
GDP (billions of ppp 1994 $)	$409	$787	$1,221	$2,024	
Average annual growth rate[a] (%)		11.0% ⌢ 8.3% ⌢ 5.9% ⌢			$\left(\bar{r} = 7.9\%\right)$
GDP as a percentage of Japan's GDP	15.8%	25.3%	33.5%	44.9%	
GDP per capita (thousands of ppp 1994 $)	$6.0	$10.6	$15.0	$21.7	
Military spending (billions of ppp 1994 $)	$20.1	$31.5	$48.9	$81.0	$\left(\gamma = 4\%\right)$
Military capital (billions of ppp 1994 $)	$72.2	$68.3	$82.8	$128.7	$\left(\pi = 30\%\right)$

[a]Total factor productivity growth rate estimated at 3 percent annually. $\bar{r}$ is the average annual GDP growth rate over the 1994–2015 period.

India

Data Sources. For the base estimates of India's GDP, population, and military spending, the principal sources are the Economist Intelligence Unit, 1993 and 1994, and World Bank, 1993 and various years. For military spending baseline estimates and military procurement shares, data have been drawn from *The Union Budget of India, 1986–1989,* and from U.S. Arms Control and Disarmament Agency, various years.

The estimates for total factor productivity have been taken from Ahluwalia, 1991.

Estimation. In our previous estimates of India's GDP growth,[9] we assumed that total factor productivity (τ) would not be significantly different from zero. In the present estimates for 1994–2015, we assume an annual rate of total factor productivity (TFP) growth of 1.5 percent per year. The zero, or sometimes even negative, TFP growth in the past was due to various reasons, including the net resource drains imposed by the public sector on the economy. Recent analysis suggests that, since the early 1980s, the situation has changed considerably. Ahluwalia (1991) estimated that the annual growth rate in TFP in the manufacturing sector was 3.4 percent per year, compared with zero growth in the preceding decade and a half. This is largely a result of economic liberalization that began in the early 1980s and has accelerated in recent years. India has always had one of the key ingredients underlying TFP growth—namely, an educated work force. Economic liberalization, which our forecasts assume will continue, will supply the other two ingredients: (1) advanced technology and (2) a market-friendly regulatory environment. Our assumption of annual TFP growth of 1.5 percent is intended to allow for these sources of future growth, as well as the damping effect of slower growth in factor productivity in agriculture. If higher or lower TFP growth rates are realized, GDP growth will be correspondingly affected.

There is every reason to believe that the domestic savings rate is likely to increase over time as Indian citizens begin to liquidate privately held assets to take advantage of better investment opportuni-

---

[9]Compare Wolf et al., 1989.

ties. India reputedly has a large stock of privately held gold, according to estimates by O'Callaghan, 1993. However, a large portion of these gold-liquidation investments is likely to go into real estate and housing. Since the available data do not permit a disaggregation of gross domestic savings into portions devoted to housing and non-housing capital stock, we have maintained the assumption used in the previous estimates for India (see Wolf et al., 1989) that the proportion of GDP devoted to capital formation will remain at 25 percent. The estimated annual increases in the capital stock are derived from this assumption.

In our earlier forecasts (see Wolf et al., 1989), India's GDP was estimated to grow at approximately 4 percent annually. In the current forecast, most of the assumptions used in the earlier forecast—including the maintenance of political stability and moderation of ethnic conflicts—have been maintained, except for the assumption relating to the increased rate of growth in TFP described above. Consequently, we now estimate that India's future economic growth rate is likely to reach about 5.5 percent, because of the higher TFP growth mentioned above.

Despite the end of the cold war, India's defense spending is unlikely to change much from its historical levels. During most of the 1980s, India spent approximately 3.5 percent of GNP on defense. This proportion dropped to 2.7 percent in 1991 because of a severe balance of payments crisis. However, with renewed economic growth resulting from economic liberalization, we expect defense spending to return to historical levels for several reasons: (1) The possibility of conflict between India and Pakistan remains an enduring facet of South Asian politics and is likely to continue into the foreseeable future; (2) although India and China appear to be moving toward closer economic cooperation, it is unlikely that India will substantially cut back its forces along the Indo-Chinese border as long as border disputes between India and China and the Tibetan conflict remain unresolved; and (3) cutbacks in the supply of arms on favorable terms from the former Soviet Union are likely to increase India's arms imports, as India turns to the West for more sophisticated military technology.

With respect to the proportion of military spending devoted to weapons procurement, India appears to be increasing its emphasis on technologically sophisticated weaponry. This trend is likely to continue. India's armed forces have decreased from a peak strength of approximately 1.5 million in 1985 to 1.2 million in 1991, but this reduction was accompanied by an increase in the proportion of the defense budget devoted to military investment. From the latest data available, it appears that approximately 26 percent of the defense budget was devoted to capital spending in 1987–1988, and this increased to almost 30 percent in 1988–1989, according to India's Union Budget for those years. Historically, military capital spending has been about 15 percent of the defense budget. While it is unlikely that India will maintain the same high level of armament acquisition exhibited during the latter half of the 1980s, we expect the average level of military capital spending to be somewhat higher in the future as a result of ongoing force modernization programs, expansion of the navy, and increased mechanization of the army. Consequently, we assume the proportion of military capital spending in total defense spending (the parameter π in Eq. (3)) will be 20 percent. The depreciation rate, δ, applied to military capital is assumed to be 3.5 percent. Two reasons account for this low rate. First, a relatively large part of India's military investment takes the form of structures (e.g., bases, depots, and support facilities), which are longer-lived assets. Second, equipment retirement rates are relatively low in India, because equipment is maintained and refurbished through retrofit of selected components and hence used for a longer time. We have not attempted in this study to normalize for the quality of military capital across countries. It is likely that such normalization would lower the relative size of the Indian military capital estimates.

Table A.9 summarizes the principal trend results for India.

Table A.9

India: Trend Results

	1994	2000	2006	2015	
GDP (billions of ppp 1994 $)	$1,193	$1,675	$2,324	$3,693	
Average annual growth rate[a] (%)		5.8% 5.6% 5.3%			$(\bar{r} = 5.5\%)$
GDP as a percentage of Japan's GDP	46%	54%	64%	82%	
GDP per capita (thousands of ppp 1994 $)	$1.3	$1.7	$2.1	$2.9	
Military spending (billions of ppp 1994 $)	$42	$67	$93	$148	$(3.5\% < \gamma < 4\%)$
Military capital (billions of ppp 1994 $)	$79	$126	$192	$333	$(\pi = 20\%)$
Military capital as percentage of that in China (%)	39.1%	54.3%	66.0%	72.4%	

[a]Total factor productivity growth rate estimated at 1.5 percent annually. $\bar{r}$ is the average annual GDP growth rate over the 1994–2015 period.

BIBLIOGRAPHY

Ahluwalia, I. J., *Productivity and Growth in Indian Manufacturing*, Oxford, England: Oxford University Press, 1991.

Apte, Prakash, Marian Kane, and Piet Sercu, "Relative Purchasing Power Parity in the Medium Run," *Journal of International Money and Finance*, Vol. 13, No. 4, October 1994.

Arms Control and Disarmament Agency, *World Military Expenditures and Arms Transfers, 1993*, Washington, D.C.: World Bank, 1994.

Bitzinger, Richard, and Chong-pin Lin, *The Defense Budget of China*, Washington, D.C.: Defense Budget Project, 1994.

China Daily, Business Weekly Supplement, June 29, 1987.

Council for Economic Planning and Development, *Taiwan Statistical Data Book, 1994*, Taipei, 1994.

Defense Intelligence Agency, *Chinese Estimated Defense Expenditures, 1967–83*, Washington, D.C.: U.S. Government Printing Office, 1984.

Department of Defense, *United States Security Strategy for the East Asia–Pacific Region*, Washington, D.C., February 1995.

Development Research Center, the State Council, *Jingo Fazhan Gaige yu Zhentse (Economic Development, Reform, and Policies)*, Beijing: Social Science Document Press, 1994.

Economic Indicators, May 1994, Washington, D.C.: U.S. Government Printing Office, 1994.

Economic Report of the President, 1994, Washington, D.C.: U.S. Government Printing Office, 1994.

Economist Intelligence Unit, *Country Profile: Nepal, India, 1993–1994*, London, 1994.

Field, Robert Michael, Jr., and Jeffrey Taylor, "China's GNP in Dollars," Washington, D.C., 1993.

Gordon, Robert J., *Macroeconomics*, New York: Harper Collins, 1993, p. 349.

Hale, David, *Kemper Financial Services*, Chicago, Ill.: Kemper, July 1994, Table 9.

Henry, Donald P., *SMOKE: A Small Model of the Korean Economy*, Santa Monica, Calif.: RAND, N-2381-NA, 1986.

Heston, Alan, "Income Levels, Growth and Price Structures in the ESCAP Region, 1960–1990," *Journal of Asian Economics*, Vol. 5, No. 1, 1994.

Hildebrandt, Gregory, Joseph Nation, Ku Shin, and Peter Staugaard, RAND research on economic and military trends to 2010 in United Germany, Japan, and the USSR, unpublished.

International Institute for Strategic Studies (IISS), *Military Balance 1993–94*, London, 1994.

Japan Defense Agency, *Defense of Japan*, Tokyo, Japan, 1993.

Japan Statistical Yearbook, 1993–1994, (*JSY*), Tokyo, Japan: Economic Planning Agency, 1995.

Jinrong shibao (Financial Times), Beijing, December 27, 1994, p. 1.

Junkuang, Zhang, "A Comprehensive Analysis of Economic Efficiency During the Seventh 5-Year Plan," *Jingji yanjiu (Economic Research)*, No. 4 , 1991.

Kravis, Irving, Alan Heston, and Robert Summers, *World Product and Income: International Comparisons of Real Gross Product*, Baltimore, Md.: Johns Hopkins University Press, 1982.

Li, Jingwen, "A Comparison of Chinese and U.S. Productivity: Sino-American Economic and Trade Relations," *The Journal of Asian Economics*, Vol. 5, No. 1, 1994.

Manpower Planning Department, Council for Economic Planning and Development, *Projections of the Population of Taiwan, The Republic of China, 1992–2036*, Taipei, June 1993.

The New York Times, October 11, 1992, Section III, p. 1.

O'Callaghan, G., *The Structure and Operation of the World Gold Market*, Washington, D.C.: International Monetary Fund, 1993.

OECD World Economic Outlook, Paris: Organization for Economic Co-Operation and Development, June 1995.

Quarterly Economic Review, Tokyo, Japan: Nomura Research Institute, August 1994.

Ruoen, Ren, and Chen Xai, *China's GDP in U.S. Dollars Based on Purchasing Power Parity*, Washington, D.C.: World Bank, Working Paper 1415, 1995.

Segal, G., and D. Waller, "China's Military Secret," *South China Morning Post*, July 9, 1994, p. 14.

State Statistical Bureau, *Statistical Yearbook*, Bejing: China Statistics Press, 1993.

State Statistical Bureau, *Zhongguo tongji zhaiyao 1994 (Statistical Survey of China 1994)*, Bejing: China Statistics Press, 1994a.

State Statistical Bureau, *Statistical Yearbook*, Bejing: China Statistics Press, 1994b.

State Statistical Bureau, *Statistical Abstract 1994*, Bejing: China Statistics Press, 1994c.

Summers, Robert, and Alan Heston, "The Penn World Table (Mark 5): An Expanded Set of International Comparisons, 1950–1988," *Quarterly Journal of Economics*, May 1991.

The Union Budget of India, 1986–1989, New Delhi: Government of India, 1986–1989.

U.N. Monthly Bulletin of Statistics, Brussels, Belgium: The United Nations, October 1994.

U.S. Arms Control and Disarmament Agency, *World Military Expenditures and Arms Transfers*, Washington, D.C.:   U.S. Government Printing Office, 1990 and various years.

U.S. Department of Commerce, "Current Population Reports," *Population Projections of the United States, by Age, Sex, Race, and Hispanic Origin: 1993 to 2050*, Washington, D.C.:   U.S. Government Printing Office, November 1993, Table 1.

U.S. Department of Commerce, *National Income and Product Accounts of the United States, 1929–1988*, Washington, D.C.:   U.S. Government Printing Office, 1988.

U.S. Department of Commerce, *Survey of Current Business*, Washington, D.C.:   U.S. Government Printing Office, various years.

Wolf, Charles, Jr., Gregory Hildebrandt, Michael Kennedy, Donald P. Henry, Katsuaki Terasawa, K. C. Yeh, Benjamin Zycher, Anil Bamezai, and Toshiya Hayashi, *Long-Term Economic and Military Trends, 1950–2010*, Santa Monica, Calif.:   RAND, N-2757-USDP, 1989.

World Bank, *Atlas Tables*, Washington, D.C., 1991.

World Bank, *International Statistics Yearbook*, Washington, D.C., various years.

World Bank, *Trends in Developing Economies*, Washington, D.C., 1993.

World Bank, *World Development Report*, Washington, D.C., 1994a.

World Bank, *World Tables, 1994,* Washington, D.C., 1994b.

World Economic Outlook, Washington, D.C.:   The International Monetary Fund, 1993.

Wu, Hai-lin, *Estimation and Application of Capital Utilization Rate in Taiwan,* Taipei: Chung Hua Institution for Economic Research, 1983.